LIVING AFFIRMATIONS

Living Affirmations: Mindful Steps Toward Inner Growth
Copyright © 2026
No part of this book may be copied, reproduced, shared, or distributed in any form—mechanical, electronic, photocopied, or otherwise—without written permission from the publisher. Unauthorized posting or sharing is strictly prohibited.

Rich Liotta, Ph.D.
Cadyville, NY
Website: www.stepsstonesandsoul.com
Email: rich@sssoul.co

Sharing Policy
We encourage you to share short, insightful passages from this book. You are granted permission to quote excerpts (up to 250 words total) on social media, blogs, or in reviews, provided full and clear attribution is given to the author and the book title. For any usage beyond this limit, please contact the publisher for permission.

Limits of Liability
The author and publisher are not responsible for any misuse of this material. This book is intended for educational and informational purposes only.

Disclaimer
While the content is designed to inform and inspire, no guarantees are made regarding results. The author and publisher disclaim any liability for outcomes resulting from the use or application of the material provided.

Published by Ask & It Is Written Publishing House
ISBN: 978-1-971052-06-9

LIVING AFFIRMATIONS

Mindful Steps Toward Inner Growth

Rich Liotta, Ph.D.

Get Your Free Gift!

***Free eBook:* How We Move in Pursuit of Our Goals:** *Sometimes We Run… Away, Toward, Astray, True*

Through the lens of soulful movement and trail reflections, this guide invites you to explore the four patterns that shape goal pursuit: running away from what no longer serves, running toward what calls you, running astray when you lose your way, and running true when everything aligns. You'll discover how to recognize these patterns in your own life and begin moving with greater awareness and authenticity.

Inside, you'll explore:

- A fresh perspective on goal pursuit, beyond strategies and formulas, revealing the deeper dynamics of how we move.
- Explorations of running away, toward, astray, and true as patterns that guide how navigate life's terrain.
- The power of the Toward-and-Away Practice (TAP), balancing what you're moving

toward and what you're leaving behind, to pursue goals with clarity and purpose.

- Guidance for following your own trail markers rather than borrowed maps.
- Reflections on preparation, rest, and rediscovering joy in the journey itself.

This ebook offers the core framework and foundational insights. It offers in-depth practices, detailed guidance, and tools for sustained transformation.

Let this be your next step. A natural companion to the mindful awareness you're cultivating through Living Affirmations.

Download your free copy at:
www.stepsstonesandsoul.com/swrebook

About the Author

Rich Liotta, Ph.D. is a psychologist, writer, and inner guide whose work arises from psyche meets spirit, and soulfulness calls. Through his platform, *Steps, Stones, and Soul,* he shares meditations, essays, and visual reflections supporting conscious living, mindful aging, and the inner path to meaning. His work is rooted in experience, presence, emotional truth, and the wisdom of walking his own trail step by step.

Connect with Rich

www.stepsstonesandsoul.com
Instagram: @soulfulseeker.richliottaphd
Facebook: Enrichments for Mind and Spirit:
www.facebook.com/enrichmentspage
Email: rich@sssoul.co

Contents

Introduction: The Trail of Becoming

"The path is made by walking."
~ Antonio Machado

In my own journey, and those I have witnessed, I've come to recognize that there are times when standing still won't work anymore. Instead, something lets us know it's time to move forward differently. Not because life demands it, but because something deeper stirs. A knowing in our thoughts, our intuition, our longings, or in our soul that movement is essential. Maybe it begins with a restless feeling you can't quite name. Maybe it's sparked by a life transition, a loss, or simply the growing awareness that who you've been and who you're becoming are asking for different things.

What I've learned is that this stirring rarely feels comfortable at first. It often asks us to leave familiar ground. It often arrives without clear directions or guarantees. But it carries a truth worth listening to. It is time to move forward with soulful awareness of what is asking to unfold.

That movement might be toward healing from something that's been carried too long. It might be a shift in how you see yourself or your possibilities. It might be reconnecting with parts of yourself that felt lost or forgotten. These inner shifts are the beginning of processes that are transformative in ways that matter most. This book is written for those moments and the journey that follows.

The whole approach comes down to something simple but profound that has guided much of my own path: just move. That phrase has echoed through much of my own life, as a psychologist, a guide, and a soul in motion on my personal path. Just move, not with urgency or pressure, but with presence and choice. Not toward someone else's vision of who you should be, but toward the authentic self that's already stirring within you.

Living Affirmations reflects this philosophy. These aren't static declarations meant to convince you of something untrue. They're living words designed to walk with you, to breathe with your rhythm, and to evolve as you do. They honor where you are while gently pointing toward where you might go.

The kind of movement I'm talking about isn't about hustle or achievement. It's about becoming.

It's about showing up to what's real and taking one conscious step at a time. These affirmations aren't wishful thinking or attempts to bypass difficulty. They are not static declarations. They're companions for the trail, messages to travel with you. Words that steady the heart, clear the mind, and remind you of your own capacity for growth.

I wrote this book for those navigating transitions, questions, and seasons of change. In my practice, I've worked with many people navigating transitions, questions, and seasons of change. This book is for them, and for you if you recognize yourself in that description. For those in the in-between places of life, identity, and possibility. For those who walk the world with reverence for depth, authenticity, and the patience required for real transformation. Whether you're rebuilding, exploring new directions, or simply learning to trust yourself more deeply, you belong in these pages.

I've never believed in quick fixes or manifestation shortcuts to a perfect life. That's not what this book offers. What I offer is something different. Instead, you'll find affirmations that have helped me and many others meet ourselves with honesty and kindness. These are not affirmations of arrival. They're about staying vibrantly alive during the journey itself.

You will also find invitations to reflect and create space for your own wisdom to emerge.

What I've found is that both provide reminders. Every step taken with awareness becomes a step toward a more authentic life. Nudges encouraging you to touch the ground, breathe into what's real, and move forward, step by step, into the next chapter of your becoming.

I hope you recognize yourself in these words. I hope you find language for what you've been feeling but couldn't quite name. And above all, I hope you feel invited to move, to be, to grow, and to become more fully who you are.

The truth is, your trail has already begun. It's right there beneath your feet.

Let's begin.

Yours in movement,
Rich Liotta

Using This Book with Purpose

This book is meant to walk with you. Not as a map with rigid directions, but as a trail companion offering guidance, steadying truths, and invitations to keep moving. You won't find wishful thinking here. These affirmations are soul-rooted signposts. They are reminders of presence, nudges toward momentum, and companions for grounded growth.

Why Affirmations Work

I've come to believe that words can reshape our inner landscape. When spoken with real intention, they transform from mere language into something that creates actual movement within us. Affirmations help us shift from reactivity to awareness, from fear to forward motion, and from self-doubt to soulful becoming. They quiet the noise of shoulds and should-nots and instead open a path toward resonance and inner truth.

Over time, repeating meaningful, well-formed affirmations can begin to reshape how you relate to yourself. They soften old patterns, reinforce what's real, and reconnect you with your deep self. What I've observed is that affirmations won't trick the mind into believing something false. Instead, they honor the mind's genuine capacity to reflect and refocus on what matters. Over time, one thought at a time, they can help you create a life that honors both your current self and the person you're growing into.

How Reflection Deepens the Journey

In my experience, affirmations are like planting seeds. The reflection questions that follow help create the right conditions for those seeds to actually grow.

While affirmations offer new language for your inner landscape, the reflection invitations at the end of each chapter invite you to explore the terrain where that language will live. They work together like breath, affirmations as the inhale of possibility, then reflections as the exhale of awareness.

What I've noticed is that affirmations alone can stay pretty surface-level. They might sound beautiful, but without reflection, they don't usually create the deeper shifts we're looking for where real transformation happens. But when you pause to explore what an affirmation stirs within you, the resistance, the resonance, and the questions it raises, so much more happens inside. You create space for genuine transformation.

Consider the difference between repeating "I trust my inner wisdom" and then asking yourself: *What does my intuition want me to notice right now?* The affirmation offers direction; the reflection opens the doorway to walk through.

I think of affirmations as helping you get oriented to what is possible. They create a kind of energized momentum that makes movement feel more alive.

The reflection questions help you take those possibilities and figure out what they might actually mean in your day-to-day life. They bridge the gap between having an insight and living it.

When you use them together, I've found they honor both the power of intentional language and the wisdom that comes from asking yourself honest questions.

Letting the Words Live

After decades of working with affirmations as a psychologist, I've found there's no single right way to use this book, or any book like this for that matter. Some people read one affirmation a day. Others flip to whatever section fits their current situation. Some stay with a phrase that strikes them as meaningful. Speak the words aloud. Let them echo in silence. Write them down. Carry them with you into your next brave step. Let them settle not just in your mind, but in your body.

When an affirmation feels too far from your current reality, try approaching it with curiosity and openness rather than resistance. You can soften the edge of resistance with gentle invitations like, "*I am open to...*" or "*I am learning that...*" I've found there's real power in honest beginnings.

Some affirmations are meant to ground you to reconnect you with presence, compassion, or truth. Others are intended to stir forward motion, offering momentum when you're ready to move. Trust what you need. I designed this book to move with, not to force anything you don't choose.

The reflection questions are doorways you can walk through if you choose, or simply spaces where you can pause and breathe. You might journal with them, contemplate them during a walk, or simply let them settle into your consciousness like stones dropped into still water. Some will spark immediate insight. Others might sit silently in the background of your awareness, working in ways you don't notice yet. You don't have to engage with them in any particular way. The questions are meant to be companions, not demanding commanders.

Let the affirmations become rhythm, breath, reflection, and part of the walk that is your becoming.

I hope these Living Affirmations can become woven into your daily rhythm, part of how you breathe, reflect, and move forward in your becoming.

I hope the reflections can become natural moments of pause for you. Times when you can listen to what's stirring and emerging inside, honoring what's real right now, and choosing your next mindful step.

I see both as invitations to move forward soulfully, different ways of becoming more authentic. They're both part of what I consider the sacred and spiritual work of showing up to your life with presence, courage, and truth.

A Personal Note

The use of affirmations and reflections is close to my heart and full of meaning. I've recommended affirmations to clients since I began counseling people 40 years ago, and I've seen their effectiveness as a change technique time and again.

But nearly 25 years ago, a crisis point in my own life deepened my understanding and appreciation of their power. I was diagnosed with cancer, and I was committed to not letting it beat me. So, in addition to moving my body, I moved my mind, utilizing affirmations for healing. I reflected on what was important to me, deciding to live more soulfully aligned. In addition to good medical care, I know what I did helped me heal.

After that, reasons to use affirmations seemed to multiply. I'd move from reflection to creating affirmations. Pursuing what was meaningful and soulfully vibrational became an even higher calling. Affirmations helped me face fears, challenge self-doubt, and lock in motivational clarity. I expanded my professional focus to include training and consulting, learning new skills, and making time for myself. Affirmations helped me there. They've helped me process grief and adjust my beliefs. Through this process, I've become more whole, and I'm still on this amazing journey.

Wherever you are starting, I believe affirmations, paired with reflection, can help you too. There's a reason they are called *Living Affirmations*.

1. Start Where You Are: Soulful Truth, Not Fantasy

"The real voyage of discovery consists not in seeking new landscapes, but in having new eyes." ~ Marcel Proust

For affirmations to feel real, they need to begin where you are, right here, and right now. I've never found value in pretending or sugarcoating the truth. They don't sugarcoat reality or ask you to pretend. They honor your present self, not as a problem, but as a sacred beginning. In my experience, every meaningful journey begins with facing what's actually true. I've come to believe that your truth, even the uncomfortable parts, isn't something to overcome. It's often a doorway into what's next. What gives an affirmation power is how it resonates with what's real for you inside, in your inner world, the terrain of your inner landscape. In my experience, real movement begins with presence, honesty, and self-awareness. Those are the inner conditions that let change take root so meaningful movement can grow. I've discovered that pairing honest affirmations with gentle self-inquiry creates the conditions for authentic movement. Presence, honesty, and self-awareness become the fertile soil where transformation takes root.

Affirmations:

- My path includes today's truth, and I walk with it.
- I do not have to be finished to be worthy of movement.
- I begin here, just as I am, without apology or pretense.
- The truth of this moment is not a detour, it is the trailhead.
- Nothing needs to be perfect for me to take the next step.
- I start from here, and every breath carries me closer to what matters.
- This beginning holds the seed of the becoming I long for.
- I honor where I am as the sacred starting point of where I'm going.
- My present reality is not an obstacle. It is my doorway forward.

- I trust the terrain of my inner landscape as the perfect starting point for my next step.

Reflection Invitations:

- What part of me is asking to be accepted right now?
- If I honored where I am instead of resisting it, how might my next step change?
- What truth about my current season do I already know but haven't been willing to name?
- What would it feel like in my body to begin again, exactly from here?
- How might radical honesty about where I am actually energize my next movement?

2. Presence is Power: The Sacredness of Now

"The present moment is the only moment available to us, and it is the door to all moments." ~Thich Nhat Hanh

I've learned the present moment isn't just a quiet space between events, it's where life actually happens. All becoming happens here. I've found that affirmations rooted in presence help us honor the richness of now, even when now feels hard. They hold space for breath, awareness, and appreciation. I've discovered that being fully in this moment doesn't stop moving. It means moving with more consciousness. I've found that presence naturally leads to reflection. It's in presence that I begin to feel what matters most. I've discovered that pairing honest affirmations with gentle self-inquiry creates the conditions for authentic movement. When I combine present-moment affirmations with reflective awareness, you discover that power lives not in control, but in conscious connection to what is.

Affirmations:

- I accept here and now, and that nurtures my power.
- My presence is the doorway to new possibilities.
- I touch this moment with care and courage.
- I bring full presence to this moment without judgment or expectation.
- The sacredness of here steadies me for what comes next.
- Deep presence today lays the foundation for tomorrow's growth.
- In presence, I discover what truly moves me forward.
- This moment holds everything I need to take my next step.
- I am fully here, and from here, all movement becomes sacred.
- Conscious connection to what is becomes my source of power.

Reflection Invitations:

- What part of this moment have I been overlooking or rushing past?
- How does bringing full presence shift my experience of the path I'm on?
- What does it feel like when I'm fully here in body, mind, and spirit together?
- What am I usually racing toward, and what becomes available when I pause?
- What can I appreciate in this breath, this heartbeat, just as it is?

3. Feel Forward: Emotions as Guides, Not Roadblocks

"The only way out is through." ~ Robert Frost

In my experience, feelings aren't detours on the path. They're signposts. They often show the way before I consciously know where I'm headed. In my work, I've seen how emotions carry important messages about meaning, pain, longing, and what needs to be released. What I've discovered is that evolution requires feeling. And feeling deeply isn't about getting swept away. It's about listening, learning, and moving with wisdom. Affirmations that make room for emotional truth help you walk with your whole self. To evolve is to feel. And to feel is not to drown it is to listen, to learn, and to move with wisdom. What I've found is this: when I pair affirmations that honor my emotions with honest reflection, emotional awareness becomes a compass, not a weakness, but a soulful guide. I've learned that feelings can become teachers rather than tyrants.

Affirmations:

- Feelings are just feelings. They can be, as I become more.
- Fear and discomfort belong on this path. I move forward anyway.
- I welcome my feelings as part of the way forward.
- Every feeling offers information. I listen for their wisdom as I move onward.
- Each emotion I welcome frees my energy to move forward.
- In allowing what I feel, I clear the way for what I want.
- My feelings are part of how I know what matters.
- I allow what I feel so I can become more whole.
- My emotions are teachers, not obstacles. I learn from them as I move.
- I trust my emotions as signposts pointing toward what matters most.

Reflection Invitations:

- What am I feeling right now, beneath the surface stories?
- What might this emotion be trying to show me about what I need or value?
- Where in my body do I carry feelings I've been avoiding or dismissing?
- How would it change my experience if I walked *with* this feeling, instead of against it?
- What happens when I let a feeling move through me without needing to fix or change it?

4. Curiosity Over Judgment: Reflection Opens the Trail

Wonder is the beginning of wisdom." ~ Socrates

In my experience, judgment closes doors. Curiosity opens them. I've noticed that judgment demands answers, while curiosity invites questions that lead somewhere meaningful. Affirmations that encourage inquiry support both reflection and movement. I've found that wonder softens your inner landscape, allowing space for mystery and meaning to emerge. Whenever I soften critique into compassionate curiosity, I find the wisdom inside me becomes easier to hear. I've discovered that pairing curiosity-based affirmations with reflective exploration creates a natural rhythm of wondering and discovering. Insight seems to flourish wherever there's space for gentle, honest questioning.

Affirmations:

- I choose curiosity over critique.
- When I feel curiosity, I trust it has something to teach me.
- I can ask questions without knowing all the answers, and still grow.
- Every time I choose to wonder, I widen the path ahead.
- Curiosity carries me into new possibilities I couldn't see before.
- My questions are doorways, not delays.
- I reflect without judgment. I grow from what I see.
- Curiosity makes space for grace to enter.
- Wonder opens what judgment closes. I choose to wonder.
- I soften critique into compassionate curiosity and listen for the wisdom that emerges.

Reflection Invitations:

- What question about my life or myself am I afraid to ask?
- Where have I been judging myself harshly when I could be wondering gently instead?
- What if I allowed more mystery, more space for not-knowing in my becoming?

- What might I learn if I softened my stance toward myself and stayed curious?
- How might reflection and wonder, rather than criticism and correction, guide me forward?

5. Authentic Becoming: You're Not Broken, You're Unfolding

"The curious paradox is that when I accept myself just as I am, then I can change." ~ Carl Rogers

You do not need to be fixed. You're a person worthy of honor and respect. Affirmations rooted in authenticity don't ask you to mimic someone else's ideal. They invite you toward your true self. What I've discovered is that becoming isn't about reaching some goal. It's about uncovering what's already there inside you, the wisdom, the longing, and the spark. We're all processes in motion, not problems that need solving. Becoming is not about achievement. You are a process in motion, not a problem to solve. I've found that when you combine authenticity-affirming language with reflective self-discovery, you create space for genuine unfolding, grounded in who you really are and who you're becoming. Affirmations that echo this truth support inner trust, self-compassion, and courageous growth.

Affirmations:

- I am not stagnant. I am a process in motion.
- My path unfolds one breath at a time.
- I am where I am, and that's worthy of respect. I am here to evolve.
- I evolve through experience every day.
- Each step I take shapes who I am becoming.
- I move in the direction of who I really am.
- I bring my true self with me, not just my best self.
- With every choice I shape a life that reflects what I most deeply value.
- My growth comes from authenticity, not performance.
- I honor myself as a person unfolding, not a problem that needs solving.

Reflection Invitations:

- What do I know is true about myself, even if I've been afraid to live it fully?
- In what ways have I been trying to fix myself, when I might instead allow myself to unfold?

- What does authenticity feel like in my body, my voice, my daily choices?
- Where in my life am I ready to stop performing and start becoming?
- What part of my true self has been waiting patiently to be more fully expressed?

6. Compassion is a Companion: Walk Gently with Yourself

"Talk to yourself like you would to someone you love." ~ Brené Brown

From what I've seen and felt, real change grows best in kindness. A harsh inner voice tends to close things down. But when you meet yourself with gentleness, something deeper softens and breathes. In my experience, affirmations aren't commands. They're companions on the trail. They travel beside you with a gentle hand, not a critical push. What I've learned is that self-compassion doesn't mean avoiding hard work. It means creating the inner conditions where effort can be both sustainable and aligned with who you are. It is clear to me that when compassion and honest reflection meet, gentleness reveals itself not as weakness but as strength, grounded in deep wisdom. Kindness creates the conditions where change can flourish.

I've seen how kindness becomes the ground where authentic transformation can take root.

Affirmations:

- I offer myself the kindness I long for every day.
- I am not my mistakes. I am the one learning from them.
- I walk gently with myself, especially when the trail is rough.
- I give myself the grace I would offer to a friend.
- I am worthy of compassion in every stage of becoming.
- The more gently I walk with myself, the more boldly I can move forward.
- Compassion is not a reward, it is a right I claim.
- The more kindly I speak to myself, the more clearly I hear my truth.
- I am worthy of tenderness in every stage of becoming.
- Gentleness reveals itself as strength grounded in deep wisdom.

Reflection Invitations:

- How would I speak to myself if I were someone I deeply loved?

- What's the true cost of my self-criticism, and what might self-kindness change?
- Where have I been harsh with myself for simply being human and learning?
- What would it mean to walk gently with my past mistakes and current struggles?
- In what specific way could compassion soften and strengthen this stage of my journey?

7. Inner Wisdom Knows the Way: Trust the Trail

"The intuitive mind is a sacred gift and the rational mind is a faithful servant." ~ Albert Einstein

In my experience, there's a deeper wisdom beneath our everyday thinking, a quiet knowing that whispers rather than shouts. The affirmations I've found most helpful don't push. They listen. They help me drop into that deeper knowing already murmuring inside. This isn't about certainty. It's about recognizing what resonates as true. When you trust your own inner rhythm, your steps become truer. I've learned that your body, your breath, and your intuition all carry messages worth listening to. Further, when you trust your own inner rhythm, your steps become truer. Learning to trust this inner guidance has become, for me, part of the spiritual journey toward becoming who I truly am.

I've found that when you combine trust-building affirmations with reflective listening, you learn to hear the whispers of your deeper wisdom.

Affirmations:

- Deep inside I know the next step, and I'm ready to take it.
- I trust the pull of inner knowing and intuition.
- I am learning to listen when my deepest self speaks.
- I listen for the *yes* within. My path reveals itself one *yes* at a time.
- My body and breath carry wisdom I can learn to trust.
- My inner wisdom leads me toward the life I know is before me.
- I trust the pull of what feels right, even if I don't yet understand it.
- My path is shaped by what resonates inside, not what pleases others.
- Deep inside, I already know more than I realize, I am open to insight.
- My body, breath, and intuition all carry messages worth trusting.

Reflection Invitations:

- What does my intuition want me to notice about my current path?
- Where in my life have I felt guided by inner knowing, even without certainty?
- What would it mean to trust my inner compass more than the noise of external expectations?
- How can I better listen to the wisdom that speaks through my body, dreams, or quiet moments?
- What part of my path feels unfamiliar, and how might I trust it anyway?

8. Resonant Action: Alignment over Achievement

"Don't ask what the world needs. Ask what makes you come alive, and go do it." ~ Howard Thurman

I've seen how action without alignment tends to drain us. But action rooted in resonance becomes a source of renewal. I've found that when your steps match your truth, they carry sustainable power. What I've concluded is that you don't need to prove anything to take your next step. Worthiness isn't something you have to earn. Affirmations that arise from inner alignment support your natural creative force and creative rhythm. Each intentional choice becomes part of the larger canvas you're creating. When I combine alignment-focused affirmations with honest reflection about what matters, meaningful action flows from inner truth, not external expectations. It is clear to me that every mindful choice adds to the life you're actively shaping.

Affirmations:

- I take steps that reflect what matters to me.
- I don't have to earn permission to grow.
- I create meaning through the actions I choose.
- My truth moves with me into the world. My actions solidify my truth.
- I walk in tune with what I believe, my values, and what I love.
- I move from resonance, not obligation.
- My energy flows freely when I act from my center.
- Each conscious choice adds to the larger canvas I'm creating.
- I trust that aligned action creates more alignment.
- My actions flow from my natural creative force and rhythm.

Reflection Invitations:

- What action or direction feels genuinely alive and true for me right now?

- Where have I been chasing outcomes instead of listening to what resonates?
- What would it feel like to move from inner alignment rather than external obligation?
- How does my energy shift when I act from my center versus from pressure?
- What kind of life am I creating through the small, daily actions I choose?

9. Whole-Self Walking: Move with Head, Heart, and Body

"Wholeness is not achieved by cutting off a portion of one's being, but by integration of the contraries." ~ Carl Jung

I've found that affirmations don't live only in your mind. They reverberate through your whole being. I've seen how real change happens when your body, thoughts, and emotions walk together in alignment. In my experience it has become clear that movement becomes more soulful when all parts of you are congruently walking the path with you. This is where I've seen wisdom integrate most fully. Pairing whole-self affirmations with honest reflection about how I'm showing up creates something beautiful: instead of just moving through life, I arrive more fully in who I am and who I'm becoming. That integration doesn't mean perfection. It means your whole-self moving together in rhythm.

Affirmations:

- Every day I bring my whole self to this trail.
- I listen to my body's wisdom as I walk.
- I let my mind rest, my heart lead, and my steps follow.
- I walk with all of me, knowing that is how I will arrive wholly.
- Head, heart, and body aligned, I'm walking toward something sacred.
- I listen to my body's wisdom, my deep insights, and my spirit's call.
- I invite my full presence to be my compass.
- Wholeness is not perfection. It reflects my integrated presence.
- I welcome every part of me into this journey of becoming.
- I arrive more fully with who I am and who I'm becoming.

Reflection Invitations:

- Where in my life do I override one part of myself in favor of another?

- What happens when I invite my heart, body, mind, and spirit to walk together?
- What does wholeness mean to me, not as perfection, but as integrated presence?
- How can I welcome all parts of who I am into this moment, this choice, this step?
- What aspect of myself has been waiting to rejoin the journey?

10. Just Move: One True Step at a Time

"Little by little, one travels far." ~ J.R.R. Tolkien

This is one of my core principles, an integrating principle. It is an invitation that runs through everything else. I've learned not to wait until it's all clear, all perfect, or all safe. Just move anyway. You don't have to leap over the canyon of uncertainty to what you dream of being on the other side. Just take one true step forward. I believe movement is sacred and spiritual. It's how we live into clarity, how we create, connect, and evolve. You don't have to leap. Just move. Let these Living Affirmations be motion-words that accompany you like trusted trail companions. I've found that when affirmations meet reflection, even the smallest steps can carry meaning and momentum. Each small movement holds meaning, power, and momentum. I've come to see that motion itself is something sacred, a way of saying "yes" to your becoming.

Affirmations:

- One honest step is enough for today.
- I don't have to move quickly. I move steadily with soulfulness.
- Movement is my medicine, my energy, and my hope.
- With each step, I write a new part of my story.
- I keep moving, shifting in mind and spirit. That is enough.
- Motion itself creates the clarity I seek.
- I trust the power of movement, even when the path is unclear.
- Each step forward is an act of faith in my becoming.
- I move because movement is sacred. It is how I say yes to life.
- I don't need to leap over the canyon of uncertainty; one true step forward nourishes my soul.

Reflection Invitations:

- What small, true step is asking to be taken today?

- What have I been postponing, waiting for the "perfect" moment that may never come?
- How might movement itself create the clarity I've been seeking through thinking?
- What would it mean to move without pressure, simply because it's time?
- How can I honor the sacred value of momentum, even when the path feels uncertain?

Final Reflections: Walking Onward

"What we plant in the soil of contemplation, we shall reap in the harvest of action." ~ Meister Eckhart

Some books get read once and forgotten. But others, I hope this is one of them, become quiet companions that remind you of what you already carry within and the possibilities that await. From the beginning, I designed this book to be a companion on your journey. Not a rigid formula, but a gentle rhythm you can move with. A steady presence amid uncertainty. A hand on the shoulder. A whisper that says, *You're already on the path.*

I don't expect you to believe every affirmation the first time you read it. You don't need to have perfect answers to every reflection. Let the affirmations settle where they will. Let your questions take time to work their way through you. Sometimes their meaning will unfold slowly, in ways you may not yet understand, and that's part of the journey. They are not spells or assignments. They're doorways. And in my experience, they are also seeds that can grow into what's already stirring inside.

These Living Affirmations weren't designed to make you believe something false. Instead, they're meant to help you remember what's already real within you, even if it had been forgotten; your capacity for growth, your worthiness of kindness, your ability to move forward even when the way isn't clear.

The reflection invitations aren't meant to solve your life like a puzzle. I designed them to create spaciousness where your own insights can emerge naturally, where you can listen to the whispers of your own wisdom, where you can discover what your next authentic step might be.

What I've noticed is that together, they create a natural rhythm between declaring and discovering, affirming and exploring, and speaking and listening. It's like breath itself, inhaling possibility and exhaling awareness.

Pause here with me for a moment and consider the following meditation. Then continue forward in whatever way feels right.

May these affirmations find you in the in-between moments,
in the hush before the next breath,
in the stillness between knowing and becoming,
in the pause where truth begins to rise.

May these reflections meet you in the quiet spaces,
where questions are more valuable than answers,
where wonder opens what certainty closes,
where gentle inquiry becomes a form of self-love.
They were never meant to fix you.
They were meant to remind you that you are not broken.
You are already in motion.
Already becoming.
Already enough.

Some days, these words will rise in you like clear water.
Other days, they may flicker quietly at the edge of your awareness.
Some days, the questions will spark immediate insight.
Other days, they will work silently in the background of your becoming.

Let them do their work without forcing anything.
Let them be what they are.
Let them travel with you.

Each breath is a beginning.
Each step a declaration.
Each question an opening.
Each moment a chance to return to what matters.

There's no need to move quickly, perfectly,
or with all the answers already in hand.

For me it has evolved to be clear that you just need to move,
stay curious, and remain open to your own becoming.

As you sit with this meditation, these questions may guide your reflection:

- What affirmations feel most alive in your body at this moment?
- Is there a reflection that keeps drawing you back?
- What shift, whether subtle or significant, have you already noticed in how you speak to yourself?
- Where do you sense movement, even if it's subtle?

Your Journey Continues

Your journey continues beyond these pages. This is what I mean by Living Affirmations, they are not intended to stay static on the page. This is about letting the words live. Letting the words breathe with you, grow with you, and change as you change. The most meaningful ones will be those that rise up in you naturally, whispered or spoken aloud, shaped by your breath and your becoming. They become part of your inner landscape, your personal trail markers. New words will emerge. New questions will arise. New steps will reveal themselves.

I encourage you to trust that unfolding. Trust your own unique process.

Even now, especially now, I want you to appreciate that you are still becoming. Thank you for walking part of your journey with these words, these questions, and these invitations to keep moving.

The real work happens when you close this book and carry these invitations into your daily life. That's where the words truly come alive.

What I've come to understand is that we make the path by walking it. We find truth by living it. We discover answers by staying curious about the questions.

Wishing you steady steps, gentle questions, and deep presence on the trail ahead.

About the Author

Rich serves as an inner guide and cartographer of the soulful trail. His unique approach integrates transpersonal and humanistic psychology with contemplative practice, supporting transformation one step, one stone, and one insight at a time. His work emerges from the intersection where psyche meets spirit, where psychological insight deepens into soulful wisdom.

Rich Liotta, Ph.D. brings over 40 years of experience as a psychologist, trainer, and consultant specializing in transformational strategies including Neuro-Linguistic Programming (NLP), Neuro-Semantics, Ericksonian Hypnosis, CBT, and Positive Psychology. Throughout his career, he has balanced scientific rigor with spiritual openness, seeing that real transformation begins with psychological understanding and unfolds more fully when touched by the transcendent dimensions of human experience. life. His work centers on a fundamental belief: people are capable of more than they realize, especially when they align with their authentic nature.

Now focusing his energy on writing, coaching, and creative expression, Rich invites readers to discover deeper layers of meaning in their own lives through his platform Steps, Stones, and Soul. His approach weaves together mindful reframing, language-based change, and systemic insight with a commitment to soulful living and conscious self-discovery. He draws from both humanistic and transpersonal traditions, honoring the wisdom that emerges when personal insight meets universal patterns of growth and becoming.

He shares photography and brief reflections on Instagram and through his Facebook page, Enrichments for Mind and Spirit. His nature photography serves as contemplative inquiry and creative expression, revealing the metaphorical terrain we all navigate in our journeys of growth.

A core principle guides his work: "Just move," physically, emotionally, mentally, or spiritually and transformation follows. This philosophy, born from both professional practice and personal experience navigating life's transitions and challenges, infuses everything he creates inspiring others to trust their own path while remaining open to guidance that comes from both within and beyond.

Through essays, meditations, visual reflections, and books like this one, Rich offers perspective and encouragement for those seeking depth, authenticity, and forward motion at any stage of life's unfolding journey. His work speaks to readers who want more than surface-level solutions, those drawn to the intersection of psychology, spirituality, and practical wisdom.

Connect with Rich

www.stepsstonesandsoul.com
Instagram: @soulfulseeker.richliottaphd
Facebook: Enrichments for Mind and Spirit:
www.facebook.com/enrichmentspage
Email: rich@sssoul.co

Countinue Your Journey

Life is a trail of discovery, and each step offers wisdom.

Stay connected at www.stepsstonesandsoul.com to receive soulful reflections, meaningful insights, and tools for conscious living delivered with presence, purpose, and a touch of nature's grace. You'll also receive updates on new books, blog essays, and access to free resources like eBooks, audio meditations, and occasional paid offerings designed to support your journey of authentic becoming.

COMPANION BOOKS

How We Move in Pursuit of Our Goals: Sometimes We Run... Away, Toward, Astray, True.

Explores the four patterns that shape how we pursue what matters most: running away, toward, astray, and true. Discover how to recognize your own movement patterns and navigate life's changing terrain with greater awareness and authenticity.

Available now as a free eBook at stepsstonesandsoul.com/swrebook (Full expanded edition coming soon).

Paths of Soulfulness: Meditations for Authentic Becoming (Coming Soon)

Guided meditations based on eight principles of soulful living: Authenticity, Presence, Appreciation, Openness, Connection, Reflection, Creation, and Action. Each meditation offers a doorway into deeper states of awareness and integration, supporting both personal insight and connection to universal wisdom.

Soulful Goal Pursuit (Coming Soon)

This book deepens the exploration begun in Sometimes We Run, offering a comprehensive framework for pursuing goals with authenticity, reflection, and soul alignment. Drawing from transpersonal and humanistic psychology, it guides you in creating meaningful change that honors both personal development and spiritual growth.

CLOSING INVITATION

The trail continues. Walk with awareness.

Get Your Free Gift!

***Free eBook:* How We Move in Pursuit of Our Goals:** *Sometimes We Run… Away, Toward, Astray, True*

Through the lens of soulful movement and trail reflections, this guide invites you to explore the four patterns that shape goal pursuit: running away from what no longer serves, running toward what calls you, running astray when you lose your way, and running true when everything aligns. You'll discover how to recognize these patterns in your own life and begin moving with greater awareness and authenticity.

Inside, you'll explore:

- A fresh perspective on goal pursuit, beyond strategies and formulas, revealing the deeper dynamics of how we move.
- Explorations of running away, toward, astray, and true as patterns that guide how navigate life's terrain.
- The power of the Toward-and-Away Practice (TAP), balancing what you're moving

toward and what you're leaving behind, to pursue goals with clarity and purpose.

- Guidance for following your own trail markers rather than borrowed maps.
- Reflections on preparation, rest, and rediscovering joy in the journey itself.

This ebook offers the core framework and foundational insights. It offers in-depth practices, detailed guidance, and tools for sustained transformation.

Let this be your next step. A natural companion to the mindful awareness you're cultivating through Living Affirmations.

Download your free copy at:
www.stepsstonesandsoul.com/swrebook

www.ingramcontent.com/pod-product-compliance
Lightning Source LLC
LaVergne TN
LVHW010941110826
845149LV00013B/2712

9781971052069